Off To The Feels-Land

Thon Piok

Library and Archives Canada Cataloguing in Publication

CIP data on file with the National Library and Archives

ISBN 978-1-55483-976-6 (trpb)

Prologue

We, for certain live in our heads, there is a world
in our heads, whether be it a world of our making
or whether be it of an independent making, we live there.
There are people, beautiful people in that world in our minds,
there are places in that world and there is good
beautiful nature and all kinds of true and genuine feelings.
A world we all long for. To live in, to be part of the residency.
A world which our beings try to achieve
day by day. Of which some do, some merge, and some don't.
A world that the poems communicate to us with
words sharper than swords and feelings that are calm and quiet.
Poems are a communication of this world in our heads to
the hoi polloi in the most simplest and feeling way.
And therefore this world in our heads is merged with
the physical world we live in and walk in.
The benefits of poetry cannot be overestimated
to this regard.

*   *   *

Poems are dominantly the provinces of spontaneous
interior experiences as well as hunted ideas and
entertaining stories carrying lessons of sheer truths.
Societies have been able to progress, perhaps to become
that world in our heads through the passage or the
communication of these pools of experiences and stories.

*   *   *

There is so much that appeals for inclusion in
a forward of a book of poems if one intends
to capture the contents within that forward.
The subject matter is vast and the condensation
is challenging. There are so many truths transcribed
and so many stories and interior experiences inked,
but there isn't one single piece of truth or

a single piece of interior experience that could fully capture and represent them all in the forward without risking being incomplete. This task has been defeating, and all attempts have been fruitless. May you, the readership, put the brains in your eyes to fathom of this world.

Off To Feels-Land

Traveler, journeyman, journeywoman,
as sure as you are now, you're
making a journey in a bit.
Besides life being a journey and
you the traveler,
you will soon go on a second trip
for a-not-so-different journey,
but a trip unlike any other you
have gone on previously.
You will not travel to cover physical distances or
change a vector a single bit,
but you will go far.
A journey comes in life, but that is rarely taken.
You'll take a trip to the land of feels-people.
Feels-people call their land feels-land,
the land of feels-people,
people unlike any you have seen before.
Feels-women are women like no ordinary
women you have ever seen.
Feels-men are men unlike any ordinary
men one has ever seen,
people who have an awareness of the existence
of alternate realities.
Women who are far from the usual, beautiful
in character as well as in self.
With big beautiful kind eyes,
fleshy sincere lips.
Men that are amply built in spirit as well as in body,
men that are far from the usual.
Tall in character as well as in the physical self,
jacked in the brain as well as physical body.
When I first went to feels-land,

the hardest thing was saying goodbye
feels-land; goodbye feels-friends and feels-neighbors.
Feels-land is a land like no other;
the feels-people are people like no other.
You as a traveler are like an individual who has set
out on a journey to a faraway foreign land,
a land like no other and people like no other.
Pack your feels-bag and your feels-luggage.
The feels-train arrives in a minute.
In feels-land, no one needs a feels-compass,
whenever a feel gets lost; they use their heart
to find the right feels-direction to the right feels-place.
The feels-people in feels-land are very sincere beings
and kind. The feels-people have an indifference
to material things as both means and ends.
Feels-land is above our earth,
hanging between heavens and earth.
The feels-people look us down earth-people
as flat as we look down an envelope
that is lying on a table.
The feels-people have bird's eye view on
fabric of society and are like "these" mythic figures
that look in so many many dimensions
and can see the whole and feels never hurt each other.
Feels-land is very different,
for instance, there are no time zones
in feels-land. Feels-time is not unidirectional and
doesn't pass linearly as earth-time does.
Feels-time is multidimensional and is spatial.
The feels-people
may exist physically in this present time
but they are actually living in
the future or past or hybrid time simultaneously.
The feels can live for many feels-days

even after they die and also the feels
could have died many feels-days earlier even if they
seem to walk amongst the living.
Consequently, there are no breaks or stops
on the feels-train.
The feels-people are unafraid of time
and none rushes or have
feels-stresses to save time.
Feels-time is not unidirectional and
doesn't pass linearly as earth-time does.
Feels-time is multidimensional and is spatial.
Feels-people have strange feels-words
for describing time that are not known
to earth-people, for example
I had one of my feels-friends tell me he would come
to visit me 'tomight'.
Tomight he told me, is tomorrow night today.
See? A night falls in advance in feels-land.
Days and times overlap on each other.
Your first few feels-days may not therefore
be perfectly ok, but what traveler
travels to a foreign land and say they're
perfectly ok in the first few days?
What traveler doesn't first find water for their
children, grass for their cattle and
what traveler doesn't first try to
understand the way of life in a foreign land?
There is no more time to talk,
and explain much, get in the train.
The feels-train leaves in a minute
May you emerge a better person after this
feels-trip to feels-people in feels-land.

Goodbye My Friend

Once again, am going away,
once again I'll have to leave
though I dearly wish to stay.
My face is scowled in grieve
that I will have to depart,
in many pieces lies my heart.

I'll have to find my things before dark,
once again I'll have to go say goodbye
and wonder whether I've left a mark.
Once again I'm going to cry
knowing that we'll drift apart after a few rings
with friends and even with many other things.

My time here will soon be done
and knowing we've been loyal friends
I'm already missing you before I'm gone.
My awareness of life's uncertainties and bends
and the fear that we may not meet again
has granted me these nights' emotional drain.

Though you may not be in my view,
my heart and my affection
will always be with you.
Heaven grant you its protection,
I'll keep you in my prayer
till then my friend, take care!

So Long

It gives me sorrow
that where I am going you can't follow
and what I hold at stake
you can't partake.

I knew you for so long,
you're not strong,
I knew you too well,
I know how you smell.

You wanted cash,
you call love trash
but love is heaven sent,
money only pays your rent.
That is why I was bereft
when I left.

I ain't chasing dollar,
I am a scholar.
That's one thing you forget
but you'll regret.

You started playing about
and inevitably sold out.
I kept memories so poignant
only to hear you were pregnant.

Well, that was fast,
given that we had a blast.
I was coming back after college…
we could do a lot better with that knowledge.

But you rejected my flower
for the ivory-tower
and now he beats you like a drum
and the hurly burly came as a rule of thumb.

Now your past brings you tears
and your future brings you fears.
You've for sure a lot of water under the bridge
But don't cry over spilt porridge.

If your plan A fail,
you've plan B, C, D...Z to sail.
Open a new page
and once more step on stage,
I know you can pay the cost
so all is not lost.

Do You Think About Me?

In my sleep, I dreamt about you
I had a dream
dreaming about you,
dreaming about you dreaming about me.
I had a dream in my dream.
You love me inside my dreams.

In the dream I was thinking,
I was thinking about you,
I was thinking about you thinking about me.
I miss you,
I miss you missing me.

You are like sorghum wine,
you and sorghum wine drive me crazy:
run like wine into my head.
How I wonder where you are
and what you are doing.
Do you wonder where I am?

Do you dream about me?
Do you dream about me dreaming about you
dreaming about me?
Do you think about me?
Do you think about me thinking about you
thinking about me?

Do you miss me?
Do you miss me missing you?

Just Don't Tell Her The truth

When you reach, look for her
until you finally find her,
and when you finally find her
talk about other things like weather
till she has asked you.
Don't start talking first about me!

Then go ahead, go ahead
tell her my life is good,
tell her I couldn't be happier,
tell her I don't think of her…
in fact tell her you doubt
I could still remember
there is someone such as her
living somewhere in this world!

Tell her I'm sober as a judge,
tell her my sanity is very clear,
tell her I have found someone
who has made me realize
why other things couldn't work!

Tell her I may not come back
tell her it's like my memory
has been wiped clear,
tell her I've found somewhere'
tell her I don't remember her!

Don't tell her I think of her
don't tell her I remember her face
don't tell her I've gone crazy.
Just don't tell her the truth!

I'm not an Offshore Fisher

In the beginning before,
before I began this fishing offshore,
in the days gone beyond
I used to own a pond
where I leapt
to harvest what I kept
if there was need
to feed

Say I was the man
who kept his cash in a can.
I grew a fishlet
in a pond by a rivulet.
It was later hit by an evil wind
and ever since it dried life's not been kind,
you know Harmattan for yourself,
how it puts plans on shelf.

Now I sit on the bank and stare
at the sea if it's willing to share.
Now I only wish
for a loathsome goldfish.
If I had never known your name,
if you had never came
I probably would never have known
fish could be grown.

I would be a happy man
being an offshore fishing fan,
but then you came
and it's never going to be the same.
I look stupid alone

sitting on this stone
holding a line
wishing for a fishlet to dine.

Hey Stranger

Hey, stranger,
you're walking away into danger,
I cannot unknow your name—
this is no longer a game.
I see past you,
Past the physical view
into your heart kind;
I see far past, behind
behind you into the bush,
into the woods where your arrows rush
beneath the Maples' undergrowth;
there's no denying we know this both!

Your Way Won't Pay

You had me at hello
and lost me at I do not blow.
I'm sorry I have to say
you are pushing me away—
but we'll do it your way
though knowing it won't pay.
This is the last time you'd conceive
of my feelings on the sleeve—
and next when you see walls
remember they are for my balls.

My Wife

My wife comes from a village somewhere
in the periphery of Mading Bor, Jonglei,
she is not here on Twitter, Myspace or Skype
or online logged in on Fb in Melbourne Victoria,
chatting endlessly with programmed digital organisms
round the clock, through to late nights—
on God-knows what social media out there…
No sir, that's not my wife, mine is in the village!

My wife is in the village, collecting firewood
and learning imperative home-keeping,
she is not in a class at Michigan being imparted
crude fabrications of sexual revolution of feminism
to liberate herself from God-knows what chauvinism!
Sir no, that's not my wife, mine is in the village!

My wife doesn't know that beauty
is achieved by a horse hair wig or
through decolorization of her melanin,
she's a stranger to the black spots that are dermatitis—
nor does she define beauty through any outward
manifestations of the ant bound body.
Beyonce Knowles is not her yardstick of beauty.
No, that's not my wife sir, mine is in the village!

My wife may have Grand Canyons of cracks
in her feet, but she is not willing to trade
that with osteopathic malfunctions of the high heel
downtown London woman, and no
she hasn't mastered the artistic
wobbling bosom motions of a good twerk,
but she sure knows how to cook and work—

and no, she's not getting inebriated
on weed on some balcony In Toronto, Ontario.
No, that's not my wife sir, mine is in the village!

A Simple Sign Will Be Fine

I will send you a sign, a simple sign,
when your paths cross.
I may not have to shout it loud
to you up in the skies like your boss,
nor do I have to descend in a cloud,
to pin point her, a simple sign will be fine.

I will send you a sign, a simple sign,
I'll send a sign when you see her, when
you meet her, I don't have
to send doves down her from heaven.
I will send a simple sign, save
myself energy, a simple sign will be fine.

I will send you a sign, a simple sign,
I will induce in you arrhythmic cardiac beat,
your heart will skip palpitations and
you will lose appetite, you shall not eat
for days after the sight of her. Ask her hand
then, a simple sign will be fine.

I'm Going Above

Nature's first gold is green
and nature's first love is a teen,
if both, you haven't been,
what have you seen?

So tonight I'm leaving behind the child—
tonight I'm going wild,
tonight I go on that track
I'll go and go and go and never come back.
Mum won't tame
and I'll never be the same

I'm going above,
I'll wait for you there my love,
you aren't paying any
I have got a penny
that I did save
when I went to slave—
and anyway we've all the time
we'll make many a dime.

Scintillate! Scintillate! Asteroid minim!

Twinkle! Twinkle! Little star
through my window left ajar,
how I wonder what you are
and why you are so far!
Scintillate! Scintillate! Asteroid minim!
My room is really dim
and my friends are at the bar
but I don't like the smoke and the tar
and I vomit when travelling in a car.
And above all I don't want to stagger
in the streets when I walk
Or stutter when I talk.

Thinking in 3D

It's a misty moisty morning;
it's a dewy drizzly dawn.
Walking to school like always,
kicking grass and snow,
keeping warm, life's good:
Eating sandwich and drinking milk,
I can't complaint. I'm walking quickly…
I have a lab to synthesize ethanol.
I'm walking in vectors, straight lines,
my path has no wavelengths
I'm walking in well described loci,
I'm thinking in 3D,
thinking in pictures and equations,
thinking about random things.
So I get caught at ethanol:
Jesus turned water into alcohol,
well, that looks strange in ~2000BC.
Wait, we make alcohol in the labs too,
I can make alcohol to regular people
at parties. Shit! I can be Jesus!
Maybe Jesus had an alkene
And dropped it into water,
hydrolysis and shit,
this guy was a chemist!

Different thoughts cross the mind.
The sayings people say about love:
love is in the air and blah blah
then I realized also,
people say God is love too,
so I equate love is in the air
and God is love.

Means God is in the air.
Simple mathematics, no rocket science.
This saying is a lie.
Nitrogen, Oxygen are in the air,
there is no % composition for God in air.
May be some Argon and mist for sure
or maybe the molecules making air are God!
Shit! God is a molecule!

Then mind wanders again
thinking more sayings about love
Love is blind,
wait a minute…
and also they say God is love
so I equate love is blind
and God is love.
Simple substraction, no rocket science,
means God is blind,!
Damn 3D thinking (enters S-Wing)!

Jesus Sermons in the 21st Century.

If Jesus was to feed 5000 men today,
the apostles would go ahead of time
to put up posters at city squares,
and even consult advertising agents to
spread the word, or enquire if
the sermon could be televised.
Besides all the cut throat competition
for audience with other celebrity concerts,
the city council would say:
you've got no license for the private rally,
no license for the fishermen,
was it Phillip or Paul?
They have arrest warrants as of now!
No license for operating open public food court,
and that fish and bread needs
testing for mercury, the city council
food authority department needs to
approve whatever you are giving
these people, plus anyway,
why use baskets?
And even if Jesus passed those standards,
a very unlikely possibility,
still some people in the crowd
would say,
'oh, am vegetarian, I will take the bread'
or 'which bread is that?
I want an Italian footlong,
am allergic to whole wheat bread.'
or 'I packed my food earlier,
I have asparagus salad,
but thanks Phillip anyway'. And some,
'Actually I have space, I'll wrap a take-away.'

And no 12 baskets would remain,
probably two baskets.
And some might take Jesus to task,
'Make us free wine, it's
going to be a long night ahead,
LCBO closes at 10pm and last call is 2pm.'
'We want champagne! Vodka!'
Beggars would start choosing cocktails.
'Two shots of tequila!
Thanks to the Son of Man'.
Others will be busy taking pictures at the event,
a selfie with Jesus or Paul, a group photo
and perhaps an autograph.
And in the evening they would take to the net.
They'd instagram The Son of Man with a filter!
Then tag Jesus, Paul and Phillip in the photos.
'Me and the apostles yester-eve
at the Shore of Lake Ontario.'
Twitter will be on fire that night,
some will go ahead to
follow Jesus on Twitter
and perhaps ask Jesus a favor to follow
them back too.
Jesus may have to follow some bitches
on twitter! They'd tweet, a tweet like
'free booze, holy booze
from the Nazerite, suck on that
LCBO and Beer Store #hastag#!'

Something's Rising

We find this out sooner than later,
there is something walking on the water
but it is not Jesus
and it isn't floating papyrus
and neither is it a pear
It's a polar bear.

This is surprising,
there is something rising
but it is not Jesus,
it's the global Celsius,
it's the level of the sea,
the data is a pestering flea.

From the clouds something's coming down
but it has no crown
it's the UV radiation,
it wants your skin's attention
because apparently you hear
not only with your ear.

The numbers are shooting to the top
and it's not about to stop,
there is no other red flag,
do not drag
there's no time to waste
make haste
be swift,
set your course adrift,
wake up and act,
global warming is a fact.
Tear down the industries

and the CFCs factories.

Down! Down bandwagoneers!

I will be passing through to the literati town
with my bandwagon tomorrow at early dawn
and as usual I know the bandwagoneers will appear
'Give me a lift! A lift!' they would shout at the rear.
Hoping to get a lift downtown in return for a cheer
and a massage of my ego along the way as I steer.
But I'll drive past and leave them the wheel dust,
to remain writhing with inner displeasure of disgust.
And to the few that would have managed to stay
back on, 'Down! Down bandwagoneers!' I'd say

"Nobody" and "Somebody"

In Thunder Bay, we wanted to create
an account on FB with the name "Somebody"
and send people friend requests so
notifications appear as, "'Somebody" sent you
A friend-request'". After they confirm the
Friend-request, it will appear in newsfeeds:
'Arop Deng and Majok Lony are now friends
with "somebody"'. After being friends, "somebody"
will like or comment on peoples' updates and
notifications will go, "'somebody" liked your
status', or "'Somebody" commented on KaBoy's photo'.
If you clicked on "Somebody's" profile,
his hometown is "somewhere"
and his birth date will be "sometime".
Then we wanted to create another account
named "Nobody" and send people friend-requests.
And a notification goes, "'Nobody" sent you
a friend-request', and news feeds like
'Thon Piok and Bior Payom are now friends
with "Nobody"'" will follow. And "Nobody" will like or
comment on peoples' statuses and there goes
the notification, "'Nobody" liked your status'
or "'Nobody" commented on your photo'.
If you click on "Nobody's" profile, his location
Will be, the hometown is "Nowhere".
Then "Nobody" will find out that they
have 50 mutual friends with "Somebody"
and then "Nobody" will send "Somebody" a
friend-request, and it will appear in news feeds:
"Somebody" is now friends with "Nobody".
And "Nobody" will post on "Somebody's" wall
and there goes the news feed: "Nobody" posted

on "somebody's" wall. Or "Somebody" and "Nobody" are chilling "Somewhere", problem Sir?

Like The Tides, fall and Rise

Sometimes life makes you sad
but there were times life made you glad,
do not cease to be grateful nonetheless.
There is a message in every mess.

Sometimes you stick out your neck
and you ought to be prepared for a wreck.
For the outcomes are infinite...
how many things can you be definite?

We cannot be gods,
and amongst us none are no dogs.
We can only be human
and amongst us none is a superman.

It is not wise to expect
that things always be perfect
but there should be that capacity
to strive for perfection with tenacity.

Expressions Are Quantized

We're given a finite number of smiles,
frowns, laughs, and cries per a life time.
Babies smile at nothing, frown, giggle and cry
at nothing. This gets lesser with time.
These expressions are given to us initially at birth
wrapped for showing people that you need
or you do give a fuck.
We can assign an initial number of each expression;
say a given number of smiles
with a magnitude of smile in tensional Newton.
Or several liters of tears or
decibels of cries and laughs.
When you've spent all your smiles and
you are out of smiles, you fake smiles to show
you do give a fuck.
You consciously pull back cheek muscles
exposing the bones that are your incisor teeth
to give an impression of a smile.
You become an Oscar nominee prototype.
The smiles are no longer floral.
When you have used up all your frowns,
you fake frowns to rise to the heart wrenching
occasion presented that one must dismay at.
You become an Oscar nominee
prototype, to show you give a fuck, before finally
your face wrinkle in a crooked submission.
When your laughs are all spent, you fake them
you become hollow; even after several rehearsals
you no longer laugh;
you do a hybrid of coughs and laughs,
like a hollow bottle in the wind.
Sometimes, exposing an array of coffee-black

molars of irregular dental formula to show
that you give a fuck.
When your cries are spent, your eyes become
dry balls that look tearlessly. You fake tears
by making a line of saliva an apparent cascade
of tears on your cheeks, or you retreat to
the kitchen to cut onions to rise to
an occasion obligatory to tear at to show
you give a fuck.
When you finally run out fucks,
you slowly grow out of these acts, and then you stop.
You give up even trying to pretend to smile,
to frown, to laugh or cry.
Some days, I have given myself a maximum
of five fucks a day…sometimes,
the last fuck is due before midday and
it's a sign of a bad day ahead.
My middle fingers get boners
and I start to type emails and assignment
with my middle fingers.

I'll clear the Undergrowth

The forest here is thick and there's no path
but I'll lead, I will, I shall go hence forth
here and clear clean the undergrowth,
I will take and I will give only the truth.
I will lead, I will, I shall lead even in death
with and in ideas, I will champion the youth
with an iron will, with an artistic strength
I will go far into the depth and the length
I will go forth and give it all my health
my life and more and when my breath
is spent this would mean me more wealth
and greater fulfilment in my inner depth!

In The Wild

Don't take your chicken to an eagle school,
it will die and worse it will die as a fool.
In the wild lions don't sleep
with the goats and the sheep.

You've A Calling? I Hear You!

Little children, little homunculi, dear
little children, who come to school here,
you've ahead a great deal of time, each year
you'll receive preparations to help gear
you to your calling, you've a calling? I hear
you when you call, I'm going forth to clear
your way ahead of you, and get you near
your calling, I'm here for that, the sphere
of life is vast, I acquaint you to it, I will steer
you where you get a call, I'll always appear
where clarity disappears, where you fear
my little homunculus, have open your ear,
I will be there, there to wipe away any tear
And remind you: that is not the time to veer
from your call, you can reach your frontier!

Who'll speak for the Weak?

At Addis, look at both the teams,
able men, in neat suits and ties, shining shoes
contemplating their dreams
of acquiring or safeguarding the power
within their reach, but none cares to speak
for the children, women and the weak!?

For all the reckless statements said
and all the sentiments aired
the women and the weak have paid
and experienced the full measure,
but at Addis who'll speak
for the children, women and the weak!?

They can go ahead continue to disagree
on all the nitty-gritties of power
allocation or on this and that decree,
they can go ahead burn time
but none is going to speak
for the children, women and the weak!?

For all the propaganda they feed
to the air and their outlets
only the weak are going to bleed
and pay the full price but
when are they going to start to speak
for the children, women and the weak!?

Is It Now?

Let's just refrain and only watch
people living in houses of glass
throw perilous conglomerates on our thatch
roofs, roofs not even of tin sheets but grass.
Then after, collect the perils into a pile
but with no insidious intent for a payback
out of anger albeit their houses being fragile.
Let's make abodes from these odds that stack
against us, we are not known for
digging two graves, no! Is it now?
We shan't, we haven't done it before
or is it now, I do not know?
There will be time to prepare
a face just to meet the faces that
throw stones, to show we are aware
of them stone throwers, of what
they intend to accomplish, whether to scare
or more, but an onlooker will lift off a hat
seeing an abode, not fragile, nowhere near!

In This Path

You would undoubtedly retaliate
and where it'll lead is inappropriate,
nine chances out of ten in this path
we would breed more wrath.
Again this path is mean
and I'll like to come clean
and wend
the holier-than-thou attitude to an end.
So I'll thwart
this vicious part
and tell you it doesn't matter
anymore who is better
because in this life
other things are worthy of our strife.

There will be Forgiveness.

With regard to the paraphernalia of daily lives,
every virtue has its penalty, or penalties.
Lucidity should familiarize one with that assertion,
loyal people get betrayed, not once, not twice
they will be no strangers to misuse or disuse,
people who risk to lead, get stabbed at the back,
sincere people are cajoled, lied to, met with
all kinds of subterfuge that they are undeserving of,
the genuine individuals are constantly under espionage.
The dangers of gentility are very pertinently
peculiar to all who partake of it. Gentility is a sort
of an evolutionary bottleneck, sounds familiar yet?
Cephalization summons extrapolation,
however, because
these people are willing to accomplish more
good for both, they know they can catch more
flies with their honey than with their vinegar;
They will try to meet their every terrible primitive
emotional reaction to these penalties with an
intellectual discipline or reason, something that
the emotionally illiterate seldom replicates,
even under several exposures to such experiences.
People who are just walking encyclopedias
of feels, ready to burst out raw, all sorts of
interior experiences without any emotional
correctness. Nevertheless these virtuous individuals
grow even more virtuous in light of it all,
a paradox that bears an equivalency in the foliage
morphology plasticity solicited by photoinhibition.
And in full awareness that there are no actual
penalties to stupidity, to stupid people,
that you can't pay them back or punish them

enough, because they are stupid
and do not comprehend or correctly interpret
any pain or verbal expressiveness upon them,
Because they are stupid, comprehension exist
in a locus that's in the blindspot of their conscience,
the emotionally intelligent is defeated, resorts to forgiveness.
Intelligence is a sort of an asphyxiation stranglehold.
It's in a lot, a straitjacket in itself.
The advantages of stupidity manifest in such,
And which the intelligent being might never enjoy.
There are penalties to intelligence, but none for stupidity.
Therefore there will be forgiveness.
Sounds familiar yet? It should! It should!

One Can Never Say All

Today I was in a scenario that normally spark
the dog in me to troll, yelp and even bark—
the scenarios I usually say out loud my mind
with the kind of verbal diarrhea short of all that's kind;
but I didn't, perhaps in the realization that-Ah holy crap!
I can never be able to say all that has got to do
with this matter out here or any other matter out there.

Or perhaps it was in realization that I could accomplish
little to nothing in following the trail that is foolish—
the trail of you talk, I talk back, you bark back, I bark back…
egos fly off handles, attitudes come in and likely an eye black.
So I didn't, in the dawn that -Ah holy cow!
I can never be able to say all that has got to do
with this matter out here or any other matter out there.

And so I left, came home, my mind searching a bottomless hole
for a way to look in many many dimensions and see the whole.
But it is misty, a vast misty hole that one can't peer clear
and I couldn't, it keeps getting bigger and bigger and I fear
that this inadequacy may hold true and that - mother of Christ!
I may never be able to say all that has got to do
with this matter out here or any other matter still out there.

It's Convoluted

Once again, they will come forth
looking sharp in very neat
suits and ties, all ready for a fierce
campaign on how to treat
the down trodden, the miserable.
They'll proceed to cheat
like they have always done before:
water, juice taps even meat.
All a grand seduction of the hoi polloi
to garner votes and beat
their other opponents in the political
arena contesting the seat.
And when one sees the cycle it reads:
beat, get the seat then eat.
None of them cares, by none, I mean
None. They'll then repeat
enough times to polish their act craft,
making it hard to defeat
them, and once again they'll come forth!

Are They Done?

Do they deserve to have another chance
to rise and to stand off the ground?
or are they done?
Should they have another time in the dance
floor for them to turn this around?
or are they done?
Should we look for longer than just a glance
for positives that we hadn't found?
or are they done?

Do we need to take back for a few moments
the swiping dictions of our words?
or are they due?
Should we take back our bile bitter comments
and back momentarily our swords?
or are they due?
Should we wait longer for any improvements
or run into wedlock with ethnic warlords?
and say 'we do?'

The Revolution

The people sang for long for fairness,
For roads and clean water, but
No fairness, roads and clean water were in sight.
They sang still until their voices were hoarse
And they became silent. They no longer
Sang but waited for fairness, the roads
And clean water. What else could they do?
They could only wait.

They waited, they waited and waited
But there were no roads and clean water
And they ran out of wait hood.
They couldn't wait any longer
And they spoke up, they demanded
They no longer sang, and they were
Threatened and scared out.
They were chased away like begging dogs
They would jog off momentarily
What else could they do?

They got scared off many times and ran.
They said sorry, they said sorry many
Times and I think they ran out of sorries
They no longer said sorry.
They watched remorselessly.
And they ran a lot and I believe they were
Tired of running so they stopped.
They no longer ran but instead
They stood still till they looked like solid walls.

They were caught and killed and they cried,
I think they cried many times and I've

Real fears they ran out of tears
And their voices were hoarse. Hoarse.
They no longer cry, they gaze with
Dry eyes and mouths agape open
But no sound. Not a sound.
That was when they fought back.
They had to. They had to and
That was the inception of the revolution

Leadership

It's about bearing an undeterred vision
for a particular mission.
It's about a clear defined reason
you strive for patiently many a season.
It`s not about the chair;
It`s about being fair.
To be ready and willing to walk
all and even beyond the talk.
It's about fitting into big shoes
and to raise those with woes.
To strive to solve any rumble
in a way that is humble.
Leaders are they whose good dream
is for the whole team.
Like a fragrant aroma of a flower
their inspirational ideas strongly empower.
To involve and raise every single one
and leave behind none.
Everywhere, even in their house
with family and spouse.

I Know Of A Place

I know of a place
Where truth dies without trace
Where a people cannot be bold
And truth is never told
Where nothing is clear
Except of course, fear

I know of a government in the dark
A government that shoots citizens in the park
Citizens whose sacrifices in war went in vain
And whose further efforts end up in pain
A government that day after day galls
The few of us with enough balls

As for us who are away
Everything is not okay
So I checked on Amazon, the price of a gun
That's heads-up enough if you wish to run
The price is well within my Budget
As you are within my target
This time am sure of your ballot
No more than am sure of your bullet

It's So Easy To Forget

We are often too swift
to forget the 'why' of this war
that's scattered and set us adrift
into the bushes and over the seas far, far...

Then fall prey of tribalism and the hate
and thereafter, live the lie
that we are out here for a country's good fate
while the spirit of nationalism choke and die

We forget the cause of the dead
or strangle and slap it in the face
for a glass of wine and a slice of bread
yet, live on with the disgrace!

We ought to come forward fair
soon we realize this life goes really fast
and all that's untrue vanish into thin air
and the stolen wine and bread doesn't last

I Reveal the Coming Ordeal

A little ahead of time I should reveal
that, when they do finally get to seal
and or actually sign this sort of a peace deal
leaders will go back to sharing a happy meal
and come out with all kinds of unity appeal
even perhaps provide few initiatives to heal
the severed relationships of the real
sufferers, but nothing would be as half ideal
things won't change, nothing! Their unity zeal
will cajole us, but buy them time to steal
this is the coming reality of this whole ordeal.

The Other Day

The other day, after walking out of my
Thermodynamics exam, I was thrilled, I thought
To myself: it wasn't strange at all, I could do better
So I went yelling, "I raped this exam! I totally
Raped this exam!" But I got weird looks. In
The hallway some girl yelled at me, "Rape is
Offensive you retarded dickhead! Gosh men are
Dogs!"
I said calm down, (could have said calm thy tits
Down but she had no tits) and I changed the song to,
"I killed that exam, yeah am a murderer!
I murdered that exam!
And I buried it, six feet under and I am going for
Its funeral right now at the bar! Ethanol it is!"
But I got weird looks again, a guy yelled at me
"Murderers aren't good son, you look normal
but you are actually a Satan!"
So this time, I stopped once more, I stopped
Singing altogether, my troll mode got slightly
Activated. "Wait, that girl called me dickhead,
That is sexist; she is shaming the head of a male
Genitalia by making it synonymous to dumbness,
And as to likening me to a dog, well that's
Derogatory to animals, such comments promote
Animal cruelty!
And the guy likening me to Satan, that's derogatory
To Satan too. Someone should stand up for Satan
He has been bullied a lot throughout history!
But anyways who cares for Satan's and males'
Consistent bullying, moustaches are dying out
At workplaces these days! SMH
Who cares for maleness these days!

So, I sucked it up, and went ahead to the bar
to drink it down, drown it in ethanol, till my
  Blood was fifty-fifty alcohol and blood!

What Art Thou Proud Of?

We speak often times
like we calculated everything
and determined what we are.
like we had a choice,
like we were consulted
on whether to be created
or not to be created.
Kicking dogs and grass
like we had a choice
to not be created dogs or grass.
Calling others potatoes or donkeys,
demeaning potatoes and donkeys
when we actually
have less chromosomes
than potatoes or donkeys.
Like we had a choice
not to be created potatoes
or donkeys.
What good deeds did anyone
do to not be created a donkey?
Even with regard to cutaneous superficialities.
Often wailing aloud
I'm black and proud
like all the races were tabled
and you made the choice
of the best race, or had
an idea of the variables
to guide the indecisions to choose
yellow or brown or white.
And ransacking the globe
because you are white,
like that gives you the right

to be demeaning.
How much effort did anyone
put in order to be born
white, black, yellow or any
other spectrum out there?
Even personal accomplishments
have little to do with thy sole self.
What good deeds did anyone do
to be born tall or homunculus?
What did you do to be born
with great athleticism, beauty
or huge tits, or any other thing
that affords you undeserved
privileges and admiration?
What did I do to have an unusual
way with words and write?
Instead of saying there's
nothing to be proud of,
I would rather have to say, pride
is baseless, has contemptuous undertones
of juxtaposition to the other being
of a different coordinate on that scale.
There's nothing to be proud of
or rather pride is baseless.
Even when it's legitimate one has to be proud,
no one should.
That you were born a wealthy American
or in the impoverished subcontinent
of India was not your working, there
was an equal probability that
you would have been born a native
in the Namib Desert in 2000BC.
What art thou proud of human being?

Bigger is Better

Size is one of the biggest factors
that has shaped the world of existence,
small is mostly dejected
because social psychology
equates size to importance,
bigger is better almost always.

The size of your country, the size
of people of your tribe or race,
bigger tribes are perceived better.
Because social psychology
attaches size to importance,
bigger is better almost always.

The size of one's biceps can be the sole
determiner of one's existence,
someone's height and body mass
gives them way or a say
in matters of significance,
tall and huge is better
because social psychology
equates size to importance,
bigger is better almost always.

The size of one's bank account
changes one's value for better,
one's net-worth is proportional to
their image and self-esteem
or confidence because social psychology
equates size to importance,
bigger is better almost always.

The size of one's GPA defines them,
their future, their existence
your GPA represents you
in fact your GPA is you,
and one's self-esteem
can be as low as their GPA
because social psychology
equates size to importance,
bigger is better almost always.

The size of one's IQ or EIQ shapes
their existence, smaller IQ is futile
because social psychology
equates size to importance,
bigger is better almost always.

The size of a man's penis is a big factor
to women in mating and existence,
bigger dick is better,
smaller dick is disaster
because social psychology
equates size to importance,
bigger is better almost always.

The size of a woman's breast is a big deal
to men in mating and existence,
bigger tits are better, smaller is disaster
because social psychology
translates and attaches size to importance,
bigger is better almost always.

The number of people of same opinion
on a matter that is a fabric of society, like religion
or political conviction pass as right

because social psychology
translates and attaches size to importance,
bigger is better almost always.

We live in utopia of size,
we live under tyranny…
the tyranny of size, the tyranny of numbers,
because social psychology
translates and attaches size to importance,
bigger is better almost always.

We've No Choice

We may have control of our feet
but not of people we'll meet.
We may've control where we grow our corn
but not where we're born—
not even to what hour of the clock,
for the creator has concealed them with a lock.
Take a good look around
then hear how you sound
for inasmuch as we may have a voice
we don't have much of a choice.

I Want to Know

Sometimes I wonder, what am I?
Who am I?
Am I alone?
Am I a clone?
Are there other ME's
beyond and over other worlds and seas?
This thought drains,
I want to lodge a few complaints
shouldn't I have been consulted
on whether or not to be created?
But there is a fundamental lie
because before I was created where was I?
Why can't I know what is ashore?
What do I stand for?
Is this strife
all there is to this life?
What is this strife going to get me?
Is that the fee,
assuming am buying my stay?
Making friends today
then fall out overnight?
Is there a bigger picture in light?
Is it bright?
Is there a cause you can fight
and in the end not regret?
And make people not forget?
What do I defend?
How will it end?
When I chase my dreams
can I trust anyone to join teams?
When and how will I die?
Do I live upon a lie?

Why can't I be quiet?
Do I need a silence diet
in my big mouth?
I ask myself, can I die a better death?
Is there a good cause to die for?
What is my life's chore?
At night when in my bed I lie
I think, where will I go after I die?
Do I have a me that isn't flesh
or is this the all me in this world's mesh?
I want to see
what will happen to the me,
the me that isn't flesh
when my heart stop to thresh!
Is there anything true?
Who is beyond the sky, or is it more blue?
Am I defeated?
Or have I been cheated?
Or is it both?
Or how is it I do not know the truth?
Is there a realm above
where there is genuine love?

Sometimes I wanted to give up

Sometimes I wanted to give up
and be a good boy
who listens to his elders,
live my life for them
plus the others
who have taken it upon themselves
to see I live my life…
particularly desirable to them.

Sometimes I wanted to give up
on my pursuits
and take their cause
pursue it, live it
regardless of my cause
and all the things I wanted to do…
what I wanted to be.

Sometimes I wanted to give up
on what I wanted to do,
do what they want me to do,
be what they want me to be.
Love who they want me to love,
chase the wind
be a soldier who fight
in other peoples' war…
let them win, let others win.

Sometimes I wanted to give up
on the things I find pleasure
and re-find pleasure in their pleasure,
the delight they get in seeing me
pursue the cause they want me pursue:

their cause,
regardless of my inability…
and remain to myself a nobody.

Sometimes I wanted to give up
and be this complete numb entity
without feelings, like a stone
See without looking,
motionless,
watch without seeing
and hear without listening
emotionless
or like the lamp, burn myself
for the delight of others…
lose myself for them.

Pick Yourself Up

You may not be the favorite son
of your mother
nonetheless, shoot for the sun,
I know how it can smother,
for sure Earth has no greater pain—-
that goes without a surprise.
But are you gonna let your dreams be slain?
I have seen many a sunrise.

So I'll tell you do not bother,
this is strange
but the absence of Carson's father
did not change
the course of his life
and you well know
it has nothing to do with the rife
Up until now.

Everything may seem blurry
mostly at the start
but do not worry
may be the horse is not before the cart
and hey, April showers
usually yield
the May flowers
in the-would-be barren field.

So remove your heart on the sleeve
and put it for tomorrow
when you will need to grieve
to a genuinely self-inflicted sorrow,
worry often grants a big shadow

to that issue
which is shallow
which you can wipe with a tissue.

The Dicken

So Geneticists recently
made a duck give birth to a chicken.
'Huh?' Yah that's right, you read it right,
Duck mother, Chicken offspring

There were questions on how to name it.
'Huh?' I know right?
That was their number one concern.
A name was their worry,
is it going to be Duck? Or chicken?
Or will it be Ducken? Dicken?
Or chickduck? Or chuck?

And how will it cry?
Is it going to Quack or Cackle?
Or will it Quackle?
"Let's wait till it grows up", they said.
''When it does, we can get to hear it then''

What about the Drake,
the Duck husband?
The father of the other Ducklings
must think his wife cheated.
Are they going to send the Dicken to it's father?
Poor Drake! Poor Duck! Poor Ducken!

Even more intriguing,
how is the Duck going to teach it how to swim?
How to walk in a straight line
like its half-brothers and half-sisters do?

Then the famous tales and dilemmas

were resurrected and put on table.
Is the Ducken going to cross the road
now that it has another identity?
without being questioned
why it crossed the road to the other side?

And which really came first?
The egg or the Chicken?
Oh! Must be the egg,
there was the answer!
The egg came first,
some other creature laid the egg.
The creature must have been a hybrid.

There were concerns too
whether McDonalds and KFC
will include in the menu
fried Dicken or fried Ducken.
This is the fate of the avian family!
Get fried.

Others extrapolated to the Jurassic park.
Some scientists threatened
to revive the Dinosaurs
and their relatives who went extinct.
They can do worse,
make a rat give birth to a human being
and continue to worry about the naming!

Lifting Off the Load

I could wash and rinse my mouth
with jiik and other corrosive detergents
that I never spoke the truth.
I could cut my tongue out gents
that I ever spread hearsay.
I could clothe my body unkempt
in sacks and in ashes lay
that my body language showed contempt.

With a red hot iron
I could poke my eyes blind
that I ever looked you down.
That I ever wrote words unkind
I could burn my fingers in pain.
for each of these has been a load
tied around my neck with a chain,
that makes me unsteady on the road.

I'm Broken Too

To my brothers
and to the others
who think am pulling everybody's leg,
whom I appear as a hen that has merely laid an egg
cackling as though it's laid an asteroid—
I want to let you know we're all devoid.

Today I would like to lay it bare,
I will put it out there
and there's no bad blood of mistake
should you decide not to give it a take.
I'll come forth clear and clean
that you may know what I mean.

I do really bad bad things
but I don't grow wings
and fly away from them—
this is my only gem,
to be true to me
even when no one can see
When you are gone
and am alone.

But your words
in my heart are like swords
I'm not an hypocrite
nor do I enjoy smite
I may appear outspoken
but am actually a person who's broken.

I stink
I drink

I drink even before I go out drinking
I take it without blinking
I have questionable morals
but it's no reason I can't give morales.

The GPA Conditioning

Yes, my self-image and
my self-esteem have been charred
by low GPAs,
yes; my self-esteem is as low
as my GPA.
Yes, endless tests and exams have driven
that fact home…again and again
and now my self-esteem is low
in fact, it's actually down, down as a carpet.
Yes, my test scores have represented me
and have informed
hordes of admission staffs and
potential employers that
I do not work hard, that I have feeble
mental potential and therefore
not worthy of consideration.
Yes, my GPA has had the final say in matters
that define me or that shape my future.
I no longer define me,
that role has been snatched
and detached from me
and has been handed over to my GPA.
Yes, my academic history
can exact trust that I simply can't.
Yes, I no longer define me, I'm defined by a GPA.
In fact I'm a GPA these days,
I'm these digits on school transcripts.
I'm a mathematical
integer these days, I'm a digit.
Yes, quite frankly since I'm now a GPA digit,
I no longer live in me,
I now live on pieces of papers,

I live online in electronic test scores,
and at times I live also on application forms,
and my life has been outsourced
onto my academic transcripts.
And this reality takes away from my life,
the underrepresentation cannot be overlooked.
It could pass as misrepresentation.
I'm not and was never my GPA.
Yes, I'm shying away from the fact that
a number on a piece of paper
can entirely
define me, or a piece of paper
should have a final say
of communicating my mental capabilities
or fully quantify my hard-work.
Yes, I run away from the fact
that these integer should
solely represent me.
I'm so much that is not my transcripts.
There is yet, so much me that
my GPA do not quantify and don't represent.
Or is the school system quantifying
only aspects they desire…
training good hands on machines
without profound reflective ability of life?
Anha, a new realization!
I see what they did there.
My school journey to be an academic
was hijacked and made
a protracted form of preparing
me to be a just good enough
corporate worker.
The school system is a synthesis mechanism
for mere corporate skilled laborers.

Corporations that have ransacked the globe.
Ok, I feel good about my low GPA now.
It was probably a bad dream
working hard in school to join that team.

Respect, U of T Students with GFs!

One girl asked me sometimes back
why I don't have a GF?
I told her: Besides other factors
such as me liking her or her liking me,
or that I'm going to break up
probably more than 20 times,
you know, I'm taking 5 U of T courses,
having a GF means: I would have to sext her non-stop,
take her out twice in a week, attend to
her erratic needs, untimely 5 hours phone calls
(Mostly nonsensical with insipid speech),
taking her to the movies, concerts, dates.
Memorize and prepare
in advance for anniversaries…
pluck reproductive parts of plants
for her occasionally
and remember to light candles at dinners,
just but a few in the endless list…
be romantic and shit in a nutshell.
It is like taking 2 or 3 extra U of T courses.
It would mean I'm taking a total of 7 or 8 courses
in that given semester,
but you see, to begin with
I don't get funding
for her, in this case, the extra 2 or 3 courses
that she is,
instead, I will even spend on her.
But the economy is bad now;

Yes, I shop at the Dollarama store.
But the other really weird thing is that
she would not appear on my academic

transcript record as a course finished
and therefore does not count
as a course towards my graduation
or towards my GPA even though
I would work equally hard on her
like any of my other U of T courses.
My timetable is full,
like packed, my school-days
are like Jupiter days, very short.
(Jupiter days are ~9hours each).
I have insufficient time.
I even want more time,
I even envision myself on other worlds with
twenty-five hours in a day, 8 days a week,
the kinds of days one has on Mars
(Dayum, men are from Mars, I cracked it).
Even now with just 5 courses, I don't pee
for the whole day
to save more time to keep up with my school.
I keep my piss till the very late evening.
7 or 8 courses will be too much and worse
if 2 or 3 will not be on the transcript record
or unused in my GPA calculations.
Instead of taking her and dropping her
and then retaking her in the summer
Or in next school year, (If she is still available
or if there is space and I'm not in her wait list)
it'd be better not to have taken her at all,
than to have taken her and dropped her.
Yes, that's why I don't have a GF,
but all in all
hats off to my colleagues with GFs and BFs.

I'm Only One Person

You see missus, I'm only one person,
assuming I don't have a clone somewhere
but even if I had, I'm still one person.
"Yes, I can see that, you are one
person, not two people or a couple of people."
Thank you for confirming that observation.
And you see missus, I can only be in one place
at a single point in time.
"Yes, no one can be at different places
at the same time though one
can be at the same place at two different times"
Again thank you for that observation,
I cannot be sitting here at the
registrar's and be at the cafeteria a mile away
simultaneously, but I can be sitting in one
place at two different times.
"Yes. That was what I said"
so what is the explanation for scheduling
me, a one person, not a couple of people
for two different exams on the same day, both
starting at 9am, but in two
separate rooms that are located five miles apart
when I cannot be at two different places
at the same point in time?
"Sorry for the inconvenience sir, there could
always be a rescheduling, here is a form
fill it out, indicating your earliest convenience."
Or, I can do the two exams if they
are on my table together,
I can write with both hands simultaneously.
"Unfortunately that's not allowed sir."

My RIP Homework Moments

Many times my mind is like a vast airport
where small and big ideas land
on and take off off of it.
Some days and times there are few ideas
or none at all and the traffic is slow and easy,
God forbid those be exams times.
They are air staring and hair pulling moments
or bald bearing moments.
Some days and times many ideas land
on and take off off of it simultaneously
and the traffic is high. There is a big ideas jam,
God forbid those be exams times too
I've many RIP homework moments then
because still I will have to make an effort
to keep track of each little and
each big idea that lands on my mind
before it takes off off of it.

This Is My Battle

Some men go to school by default,
others don't and it may not be their fault—
I don't mean to assault

Some men die of gonorrhea
some die of diarrhea
and yet others for an idea.

There's no death to rejoice
but a noble voice
is sure a great choice.

This is the battle I chose
for forty times I've fallen close
and for forty times I rose.

And I made no sound
I've searched around
but I haven't found.
A straw to clutch
and as such
it's made the pain too much.

The battle lines were drawn
I could not back down
it's the least am known.

In sight there were no lights
for forty days and for forty nights
still I put up really good fights.

I couldn't even pee
I kept being a bee

for honey I couldn't see.

I knew not which way
but it was okay
I kept the surge anyway.

In the same path
for all what it is worth
I knew from Alice on this earth.

As long as you take a dose of the atmosphere
if you need to go anywhere
any road doesn't matter from here.

Maybe it will pay
some foul day,
maybe not, we cannot certainly say.

But there is nothing to prove
I shall have made my move
from where someone will improve.

I shall have done my part
in pushing the cart
before I depart.

It Was Not That Time I died

I have lost my mother's watch
for close to a quarter century, parentless
but it was not that time of parentlessness I died
though still, I did die a little bit then.

I've gone out wandering in the bushes
for days and nights unclothed, endangered in the wild
but it was not that time of wander I died
though still, I did die a little bit then.

I have measured out my life with
three to four cups of maize grains, I starved
but it was not that time of starvation I died
though still, I did die a little bit then.

I have chased my dreams, dreams that were
winging fantasies and lost them all but feathers
but it was not that time of dream loss I died
though still, I did die a little bit then.

I've gone out to boldly take on life even with
my skin assigned a horde of stereotypes and also
it wasn't that time of cutaneous superficialities I died
though still, I did die a little bit then.

Even, that the summation of these bits
of death were sufficient to kill me, I did die from the
daily awareness of consciously authored pains. It was the
last straw, though still, I did die a little bit then.

Think Britain, Reflect America.

Europe's Britain go to bed this afternoon,
North America's States go to bed this
evening in the light of the moon,
and before you all fall asleep,
think, reflect on what you did all day long,
think how many friends you will keep
and do count how many friends you've made.
Think about what you did the previous
day, reflect on how many friends you bade
farewell, think back in time if need
be, to the past few centuries and all the way beyond.
Then, itemize many a good humane deed
you did in those times of your past,
America, think of kingdoms bigger and powerful,
think of ancient Egypt, Greece and think at last
how they are no more, think kingdoms rise
and think kingdoms fall to ruins too.
Soul-search how the previous day you were unwise
because when you snore in the midnight, Asia, Africa wakes.

The Best West

So here we are in the west,
I sought to tell myself why it's the best
how it's worth the medical test
and why it's yearned by the rest
where necessities lack;
Come and then never go back,
why opportunities are here
but are not to be found elsewhere!
We have to come out of the cover
because the dog days are over.
We've different blood groups for our endeavors,
not for mosquitoes to enjoy different flavors.

I'm Going Back Home

I'm a nobody
staying nowhere,
I stay up all night
I have no life,
I see no light,
my life is all bills,
these bills will kill me.
I have no light,
I'm going back home
to find my life
among our people,
I want to be somebody!

I'll Use a Long Knife

When life shall have taken all my youth
and given me in exchange its truth,
when am no longer a greenhorn,
I will return to the very place I was born
and sing poetry aloud to my brethren
and to all the little children.

I will sing it to children whose hearts are soft as satin
I will not pour my new wine into old wineskin
I will keep my poetry for donkey's years
I will not waste it on deaf ears,
the wisdom of this life
is that when you're after the devil use a long knife.

They'll Come Look for it

Should I post them?
Yes, father, say yes!
This here is gem,
he who really cares
about people, about friends
for sure shares—
and how would I have known
if it wasn't shared to me?
If in the beginning I weren't shown?

Should I share them?
No! No my son! You shall quit!
Poetry is not to be sun dried
this to poetry doesn't fit—
Poetry has its firm charm,
they'll come look for it
whose hearts seek warm
It's to be found by men from the East
or like Jacob for Rachel on the farm.

I Will See You There.

Let me tell you people, the village is warm
everything is organic, well, ok but
almost everything, look the food on the farm
is organic, less fertilizer, less GMO.
The milk, the sorghums and the corns
are all organic, even the people are organic.
The music is made by blowing horns.
See? Even the music is organic too!
The drums too are made of wood
and the sticks and the leather are organic too.
Let me tell you people, the village is good.
The sleep is serene and biphasic,
the lighting is sun by day and by night moon,
look, even the light is organic too.
So if you can, let us go back to the village soon.
The village is good, the children are children
the women women, and the people how they smile
is organic. In the village the people are people.
I'll see you there, in that village by the Nile.

YOU

You are not simply you,
here is a mirror, show me your mothers
your father, sisters and your brothers
and I will show you you, yes!
You are them and they are you.

You are not quiet you,
here is a mirror, show me your friends
and point me those they make amends
and I'll show you you, yes you're right!
You are them and they are you

You will never simply be you,
here is a mirror, show me your teachers
and tell me who are your preachers
and I'll show you you, yes you're right again!
You are them and they are you.

You are actually not you,
here is a mirror, you're the air that runs around,
you are where you walk on the ground,
you are everything you ever touched, saw, heard, yes!
You are them and they are you

In fact there is really no you,
from when you stepped out your mother's womb
until the day you will be finally laid in your tomb
don't forget that you are everything you can think of!
You are them and they are you.